BY KIDS
FOR KIDS

A collection of original
MONOLOGUES
for Kids and Teenagers
6 to 18 Years Old

Edited by
CATHERINE GAFFIGAN

Excalibur Publishing
New York

Published by:
Excalibur Publishing Inc.
511 Avenue of the Americas, PMB 392
New York, NY 10011

Cover design: Peter J. Byrnes

Library of Congress Card Cataloging-in-Publication Data

By kids, for kids : a collection of original monologues for kids and
   teenagers 6 to 18 years old / edited by Catherine Gaffigan.
       p.   cm.
   ISBN 0-9627226-8-5 (pbk.)
   1. Monologues--Juvenile literature. 2. Acting--Juvenile
literature. 3. Children's writings, American. [1. Monologues.
2. Acting. 3. Children's writings.] I. Gaffigan, Catherine.
PN2080.B95   1994
812'.04508--dc20   93-31562

Printed in the United States of America

10 9 8 7 6 5

*This book is dedicated to the
memory of my mother
Catherine Murphy Gaffigan*

*Who introduced me to the
joy of reading and love of
the spoken word*

Table of Contents

Monologues for Girls or Boys

INTRODUCTION

This book is for actors from age six through eighteen. You could be just a beginning actor, or you might already have experience at auditions or acting in plays, television or movies. In either case, you will find monologues here which you can use for auditions or just for practice. The age ranges are flexible, so read all the monologues a bit younger and a bit older than your actual age.

All of the monologues are *original*. Each one was written by someone who tells about something or someone that matters to them. And they wrote it down. Many of the stories are true. Some are funny, some are sad, some are weird. You are sure to find something that you can use, and will probably like several of the pieces. You certainly could work on more than one, but it's best to work on one at a time.

◆ *What is a monologue anyway?*

The word "monologue" has come to us from the Greeks: "mono" means single or alone, and "logos" means to speak or read. So a monologue is a story which is spoken by one actor. That actor can tell the monologue within a play where there are other characters. Or an actor can perform a whole play by himself or herself, which makes the play just a long monologue.

◆ *Who needs a monologue?*

Usually, people learn monologues so that they can use them to audition for parts in plays. As an actor, you will perform your monologue for Directors, Casting Directors, Producers and Agents.

◆ *What do Directors and Producers do?*

Directors and Producers hire actors to be in plays,

3

films and television. If you are auditioning for a school play, the Director or Producer could be one of your teachers.

◆ *What do Casting Directors and Agents do?*

Casting Directors and Agents send actors to see a Producer or Director. In order to get to know you first, the Agent or Casting Director talks to you for awhile, then usually asks you to perform a monologue.

◆ *What is the reason to perform a monologue for a Producer, Director, Agent or Casting Director?*

All of these people will watch you perform your monologue to find out if they can hire you to act in a play, movie or television show.

◆ *Where will you perform your monologue?*

Very often, you will perform a monologue in the office of the Agent or Casting Director. Some people call that "office acting." If you audition for a Producer or Director, you will probably perform your monologue in a rehearsal studio or in a theatre.

◆ *How do you choose a monologue?*

Read through all the monologues for your age group in this book. If you need help, have someone read along with you. Read carefully and slowly. Once you've read everything, see if you have a favorite or several favorites. It's very important that you like the story that you are going to act. If you like the story, you will have more fun telling it to others. And that's really what you do when you "act" a monologue — you tell the story.

◆ *How do you get ready?*

After you choose your favorite monologue, then you have to memorize it — you have to learn it by heart. Next you have to decide who you want to tell the story to in your imagination. That means you choose or make up a person or an animal who you are talking to when you say the monologue. For example, in your imagination, you can be telling your monologue to your Mom or Dad, your best friend, your teacher, your dog or even a space alien.

♦ *What do you do after you learn the monologue by heart?*

Once you have memorized your monologue and decided who you're talking to, you have to rehearse. That means you must practice your monologue until it becomes very easy for you.

♦ *Why does an actor rehearse?*

Acting is just like school work or sports or learning to play a musical instrument — it takes practice. You have to do your homework ahead of time. That way you are sure to do your best at an audition.

♦ *How do I rehearse?*

Stand by yourself in the front of the room. In your imagination, think of your Mom, your teacher, your dog or your best friend (whoever you've chosen), and tell the story to that person or pet or alien. You should rehearse at least ten times so that you get comfortable and are having fun acting the monologue. You can rehearse alone at first, but be sure to do your monologue at least a few times in front of a real person, so that you don't get scared the first time you face a live Casting Director. SPECIAL NOTE: DO NOT EVER REHEARSE IN FRONT OF A MIRROR.

♦ *When I finish rehearsing, what next?*

Once you have done your homework, you are ready to act for the Agents, Directors, Casting Directors and Producers.

♦ *What should I expect to happen as a result of doing an audition?*

Remember that a monologue is a stepping stone — acting a monologue is a way for you to show someone what a good actor you are and that you have done your homework. But the main point is, a well-rehearsed monologue is a very good way to get an acting job, a good way to "land the role."

♦ *What is a "successful" audition?*

Think of it this way: *Every audition that you do is successful if you learn something from it.*

First, if you do your monologue and you get the part, then your audition is successful in the obvious sense.

Second, there are many other opportunities to be successful. For instance, when you do your monologue for many different people and many different parts, you develop confidence and what is called *poise.* That means you know how to handle yourself at other auditions. So your audition has been successful if you are stronger and more experienced. You know what to do and what not to do. Plus, you start to realize what to expect when you go into the office or theatre to do your monologue.

Third, there will also be times when you feel that you did a very good audition — your monologue went very well, and you enjoyed performing it — but you didn't get the part. Often, the reason you don't get a part has nothing to do with how well you performed your monologue. You could do it perfectly — people might laugh if it's funny or look moved if it's sad. But you might not "match" with the person who is going to play your sister or your mother. Or the director might want someone shorter or taller or fatter or thinner. You have no control over the situation, and you should NEVER ASSUME something is wrong with *you* because you don't get a particular role.

Fourth, your audition can also be considered successful if it causes an unexpected result. For instance, you might say to yourself afterwards, "I don't really like doing this, and I don't want to do it anymore right now." If you feel that way, it's a good idea to be honest with yourself and not make yourself unhappy. You also leave the door open for thinking about acting later when you are older, because you can always change your mind.

And finally, an audition can be considered successful if it causes you to ask yourself this question: Why should I be acting in the first place?

The reason to be an actor is because you absolutely *love* doing it, and you enjoy it immensely, the way you enjoy a challenging game. In other words, do it for yourself. If you think of acting as a way to please your parents or to support your family, you will make yourself very unhappy. So ask yourself, "Would I rather be doing this than anything else at this moment?" If the answer is "absolutely yes," then you should go ahead and do it.

Also — and this is equally important — you should keep up with your other interests: your schoolwork and "team" activities like the school paper, sports or the Scouts. Remember — an actor has to be a well-rounded person, too!

We wish you enjoyment in your monologue work, and great success in your auditions!

In acting, it is traditional for actors to say "break a leg" to each other just before the play begins. It means, "good luck and have a wonderful time acting."

So — break a leg!

Acknowledgments

My special thanks to my colleague and publisher, Sharon Good, and to all of our contributing writers in this volume who have shared *their* talents so generously, and to the teachers, administrators and family members who helped us find our writers.

Catherine Gaffigan
New York City, 1993

Monologues
for
Girls

The Lazy Beach Party
by Melissa Ebbets

I was having a beach party. We all were talking, swimming and playing games. Most of the kids were swimming. I was talking to my friend, Valerie, about going back to school.

Me: So, are you ready to go back to school?

Valerie: Yeah, I guess so.

Me: So, what did you get for school?

Valerie: Glue, pencils, scissors, a back pack, pens, a crayon box, crayons and a folder. And what did you get?

Me: Same thing. Did you get any clothes?

Valerie: Yes. Did you get any?

Me: Yes. I got a top and skirt, long pants. But nothing much.

Then someone yelled, "Help! There's a shark out here." Everyone came running out of the water, and they all had cuts and bruises. I said to everyone, "Do not go out in the water again tonight. Got that?" Everyone said yes. So then the First Aid Squad came. Most of my friends had to go to the hospital. They had broken arms and legs. I said to Valerie,

Me: Do you think they will be back before school?

Valerie: No, they have a lot of recovery.

Me: Yeah. I guess so.

Valerie: Bye, now.

Me: See you in school.

Valerie: Okay.

And that's the end!

The Magic Book
by Saara Pritchard

One day, I was reading a book. It was so fun! At my favorite part, I magically went into the book. Crash! I fell in a tree. I could see the whole forest. Suddenly, I fell down out of the tree. I saw a horse standing in front of me. It was a chestnut color and had a golden mane and tail. It said, "Get on my back, and I'll take you to a good place where there are a lot of me." The grass was very green. When we got there, I saw a lot of horses, and they were so beautiful. Then the most beautiful horse said, "Let's go." "Go where?" I said. "To a beautiful castle."

When all the horses and I got there, I got off the horse I was riding. I went inside the castle and saw a very beautiful princess. She had golden hair and a golden dress. She said, "Come, you must be tired and hungry." She gave me some cookies and took me to my room. It was true that I was tired. I went to my bed and ate the cookies. Then I heard the princess singing a beautiful song. She was singing a lullaby. When I came in, I saw her with a little baby. I said, "What is the baby's name?" The princess said, "Aurora." I said, "That's a nice name." "Thank you," she said.

One day, she said to me, "You must go home." I was sad, but I had to. I went to the stable. I got a horse and went back to my favorite part in the forest, and I was back on my bed. It was night. I put the book away and went to sleep. The next morning, I got up and took a shower, brushed my teeth, washed my face, got dressed and went to school. I told all my friends what happened. They did not believe me. I told my Mom and Dad. They did not believe me.

All About Alex
by Betsy Kagen

My big brother's name is Alex. He's very, very strong. My brother is nice some of the time. He's in high school. He's seventeen, and he is crazy about basketball. Alex has brown hair and green eyes, and that's about it. But when he is in the sun, it looks really blond. When Alex comes home and I am watching TV, in the most important part, he interrupts me. I say, "Alex, stop!" He doesn't stop. I yell, "Mom!" Then Alex stops.

If Alex is ever late for washing the dishes, I yell "Alex, front and center!" He comes running. If Alex is not there when I want to play with him, I go into his room without knocking and say, "Play with me or else." He laughs. I scream. Mom comes running and says, "Alex, don't laugh at your sister." I stick my tongue out, and I get away with it.

But life's not that easy. My brother just has to finish his English paper. I get in trouble with my Mom, not letting him use my computer. It's my computer! She said I should share. I hate it. When Alex had his operation, I was totally jealous. Not jealous that I didn't have the operation. I was jealous, because he got all the presents.

Oh, and Alex has a mysterious girlfriend. They met in Mexico. I think they really like each other.

We're going to get a dog. Alex wants to name it Mindy, because that's his girlfriend's name. Love connection. She is nice. She says, "Hi, Betsy." She has really high heels.

The New Neighborhood
by Sharon Good

We moved here when I was five. Well, four-and-a-half, really. Before kindergarten. I was born in Brooklyn and lived there all my life until then. Nobody in my old neighborhood went to preschool, so we pretty much stayed home, and my little sister was the only kid I had to play with — my mother didn't think it was safe for us to go out alone. I was kind of nervous about meeting new kids.

Maybe that's why I got sick the day we moved. I had a fever, and I didn't feel too good, but we had to move that day, so we did. My mother wrapped me in a blanket and carried me out to the car. It was spring, so it wasn't too cold. Then we drove to our new house. It was pretty nice. A big, red brick house. The good thing was, I got my own bedroom, so I wouldn't have to share with my sister anymore. I still had the fever for a couple of days, so my parents let me lie on the living room couch and look out the bay window. It was so different from Brooklyn. The street was much wider and the houses were all new. And there was only one family in each house. My parents said there were a lot of kids I could play with, but I was still scared about meeting them.

Well, my fever got better, and I finally had to go out. My mother took me out on the front porch and told me where all the kids lived. This one girl, Cynthia, lived right across the street, and she was on her front lawn playing with her dog, Delilah. She waved at me, and I waved back. My mother gave me a little push and told me to go over and introduce myself. I did, and she turned out to be pretty nice. She had two new dolls, and she let me play with one. She became my best friend. She's really nice. I have lots of friends now, but I still like Cynthia the best.

Self-Defense
by Christine Hutchinson

So what, my brother beats me up. He's just fooling around. He gets mad at me sometimes, and we both know that. And if he does really hurt me, he'll help me feel better. My brother's very protective, and he really does take care of me. If anyone tries to bully me around, my big brother's always there to set them straight. He teaches me self-defense. And with him beating up on me every day, I've gotten stronger, and I've learned to protect myself a little. But I'd rather have him protect me. He may not admit it, but he loves me. He doesn't tell me, because he doesn't want to be a dweeb. I love him, and I hope he'll be my protective big brother forever.

Grounded
by Lindsay Froelich

I can't believe she did that! My most favorite thing in the world, my bike, was ruined yesterday by my older sister, who didn't even ask to use it, but she did anyway. She rode it and fell five times, crashed thirteen times, broke the spokes and wheels, bent the handle bars, broke the seat, and then it all collapsed on the ground. She was too far from home to walk, so she called from a friend's house and asked Mom to come with the car and get her. When I heard, I was so mad. I was glad she got grounded and that she has to save money for a new bike for me. When I get the new bike, she better not try that again! Or else!

A New Baby
by Christina McCullough

A few weeks ago, my Mom was going to have a baby. My Mom was so thrilled about having a baby, but I was not thrilled. I just knew the baby will cry all night. And maybe the baby will have all the attention. That means war!

Then one day, the time finally came. My Mom was calling me. When I got to the bottom of the stairs, she was holding my coat. That meant she was ready to go to the hospital. My Dad and I were waiting many hours. Dad talked to me and bought me juice. Finally, we both heard the door open. My Dad and I jumped up as quick as we could, and the nurse was smiling. We waited, and then we could go in, and I heard my mother saying, "It's a girl, it's a girl!" My Dad and I went home as fast as we could to set up the baby's room.

In a few days, my Dad went back to the hospital to get Mom and my new baby sister. He got me a babysitter. I just sat on my bed. My babysitter came into my room to talk to me about the baby. Then suddenly, I heard voices. I was just sitting on my bed, so my babysitter opened the door. All of a sudden, I heard my Mom's voice. I jumped up and ran downstairs. Then I saw my Dad paying the babysitter. I ran into my Mom's arms. We both covered each other with hugs and kisses.

My Mom and Dad named the baby Karen. I kissed my little sister. She was very sleepy. It wasn't that bad after all!

Spearmint
by Nat Van Order

I've been in elementary school for five years and three months, counting kindergarten. So that makes five years and three months that my teachers have scolded me for daydreaming instead of paying attention. Then when I go home, my mother scolds me for dreaming. When I get an important idea or a different kind of thought, I like to wonder about it. Sometimes I think about inventing something, or what's inside a squirrel that makes it so fast and able to jump and climb in trees the way it does, or I think about circles. I don't like circles. They roll away. Sometimes, I just say "spearmint" over and over to myself. "Spearmint." I like to say "spearmint."

It's not just my dreaming. My mother says my teacher, Miss Howell, complains that if I'm not dreaming, I'm talking to other kids when she's trying to teach. Well, when you're in fifth grade, it hurts your body if you have to sit still too long. I like Simon Says, because I can move my arms and legs playing Simon Says. I can pretend that I'm in places all over the world playing Simon Says.

My mother had a conference with Miss Howell and the principal. Right away, I know I'm in deep trouble, because "conference" is not a good word for a kid in school. My mother told me that they've decided to put me in a different class. But it's not the way it sounds. What they mean is, different grade. I've only been in fifth grade for three months, and they're talking sixth grade already! I told my mother, I don't want to be in Miss Robinson's class. She's the sixth grade teacher. She yells all the time in her loud voice. If I'm put in Miss Robinson's class, I'll walk out and go home the way I did in kindergarten. In kindergarten, I stayed until I had to go to the bathroom, and then I left and walked home. The toilet in kindergarten had drops on the seat. I didn't like it. Personally, the thing that worries me the most about Miss Robinson's class is, how can I think in there? If she talks so loud, how can I dream there?

My mother had another conference. So what do you think they came up with? They put me in seventh grade! They have Social Studies in seventh grade. I never heard of Social Studies before. I really have to pay attention to catch up with the seventh grade kids. And they whisper things to each other and won't share their secrets with me — they say I'm too young.

So now I dream about recess. I have to find a buddy to play with at recess. Then we can whisper together.

JoJo's Ghost
by Priscilla Cruz

It was one rainy day. My father and I were watching TV, my mother was cooking dinner and preparing for the next day. And all of a sudden, the lights went out, my mother screamed, my Dad panicked. I did also. I turned the lights back on, and then we all ran to the back room and saw a black bag. My Dad opened the bag and saw that it was my friend, JoJo. But nobody knew why he had kill him own self by a belt, because he wasn't the type that like to kill people. Then my sister called the police, and my Dad was trying to get the belt off him, and JoJo fell on the floor, and my Dad got him breath again. But the police came and handcuff him and took him to this place that would take care of him. Then I went upstairs, and I jump on my bed, and I felt a hard thing. I turn the light on, and I saw this man laiding there, and he look like he was going to do something to me. So I ran back down the stairs, and my family was gone, so I said to myself, "They will come back." So I waited for more than one hour. Then I started to said to myself, "I have to get out, because there something worrying me." So I left the house, and I never saw my family again.

One Saturday morning, I woke up. It was snowing, while I was looking out the window. I saw a person that was sitting on my stoop in the snow, so I ran down with my robe and jacket on. I got outside, and I try to wake him up, but he would not budge. So I went inside, and I called the hospital. And then they came, and one of the doctors said to me, "Isn't that JoJo?" I said, "Yes, that him. But how did you know?" The doctor said, "He's been in hospital five time." I said, "For what?" But before he could tell me, I heard a loud noise, and the doctor turn back, saw

JoJo laiding there.

And so we took him in the ambulance, and we got to the hospital. The name of the hospital was Brooklyn Hospital. So I was walking up and down the hall, and I saw the man that was in my bedroom, and I screamed! Then the doctor came, and I ran to him, and I said to him, "Look over there." And he said, "There nobody there." And then I ask how's JoJo, and Doctor Moore didn't said nothing. I knew that JoJo was die. Then I went home and ran to my bedroom. I stayed there all night crying. Then when I woke up, I smelled something very good. It smelled like muffins that just came out of the oven and fresh orange juice, and it also smelled like a fresh pick rose from a garden. I put my robe on and went downstairs and saw Doctor Moore making my breakfast. And I ask why he did this for me. He said, "Because what happen to JoJo. Okay?" Then he left my house.

So that afternoon I went out and took a walk for three hour. Then that afternoon I went home, and I was watching TV. I heard the door open, and I said to myself, "How did the door open by itself? It's not windy out." So I went to check the back door, and that wasn't open. So I check the front door was open, so I closed it. And then I look around the house to see if there was somebody in the house. But when I look around house, I didn't see anybody in the house. So I went back to watch TV. But I went . . . I went to sit down, I heard this man was calling my name. "Priscilla . . . Priscilla."

Class Report
by Lauren Weinrich

It was in fourth grade. My teacher, Mrs. Pinnow, told the class that we had two weeks to research and prepare a dress-up book report on a famous person. Well, you see, my ambition when I grow up is to be a singer, so I decided to do a report on a singer.

The next day, I went to the library to find someone I could easily dress up as. I found books on Dolly Parton, Whitney Houston, Vanessa Williams and Madonna. Thinking carefully, I realized that I'd like my report to be fun. So, I decided to be Dolly Parton. The next day, I picked out my costume. A denim skirt, a denim vest, and a Western shirt seemed like the perfect touch. I added some balloons to fill out my chest like Dolly Parton, and I was ready.

I could hardly wait. Finally, the day of my report came. I walked to school with my costume in a bag. When the teacher called me, I literally jumped out of my seat and ran to the bathroom to change into my costume. I got into my outfit, blew up my balloons, and walked back to the room.

When I got to the classroom, I realized everybody was staring at me. I was about to die! But I bravely walked to the front of the room. When I finished, I realized that people were laughing, not because of my report, but something else. A friend pointed down. I quickly looked down, realizing that one of my balloons had fallen to the floor! I blushed and tried to think of something to say, when an idea came to me. I said, "Thank you for being such a great audience," and crushed the fallen balloon with my foot.

Everybody laughed, but I think it was with me, not at me.

Being Weird
by Jami Noël English

Okay, I can't help it, I'm weird. Instead of going to school in jeans and a T-shirt, I show up in bell bottoms and a grunge tube hat. That's me. That's who I am. Individuality is cool. It sort of comes out and says, "Hey, people! I'm me, and if you want to go around being like every other boring person in this whole boring world, go ahead, be my guest. But don't interfere with me trying to be myself."

I'm not trying to make a statement or anything by being weird. I mean, I don't go up to people and say, "Hi, I'm weird." But I certainly don't go up to people and say, "Hi, I'm just your everyday person." If you get to know me, you'll see that I'm not the normal kid that meets the eye.

I think really strange thoughts. In fact, some of my thoughts are really intense. When I'm in bed, my thoughts take control of me, and they scare me. I'll think that there are monsters in my room, or even worse, that my thoughts are the monsters and that they're going to devour me. When I wake up, it seems silly, like little kid stuff. But if I'm not careful, my thoughts can really take control and make me very tense. I can sometimes imagine things that are nice, exciting, pretty, like a vacation, a field of flowers, things like that. So the intense thoughts are faded for a time. But they never go away completely. There are monsters everywhere.

If I Had Aladdin's Lamp
by Ida Barron

If I had Aladdin's lamp, I would wish upon it to be a woman hero of my country. I like to read, and I have read about a lot of men who went out on the battlefield and saved their country. But there is not much about the women. They do tell about Joan of Arc, but she was not well treated, after all.

Imagine leading a regiment bravely toward the enemy. Of course, I know I might be killed or be caught and sentenced to die before a firing squad. But then I would say grand and unforgettable words, like the words that the history books say that Nathan Hale said. Then everyone would remember me. I would count.

There must be many unsung women heroes of every country. I want to be a sung one.

Report Card
by Sharon Good

I hate my father. I just brought home my report card. I had straight A's and one B. One B. Do you know what he said? "How come you got a B?" Not a word about all the A's. It makes me so mad. My friend Ellen's parents give her a dollar for every A she gets, but I get yelled at if I get a B. It's not fair.

Sometimes I don't think my father likes me very much. If my brother comes home with all C's and maybe a couple of B's or A's, my father tells him he did a great job. When I complain, he tells me that they don't expect as much of my brother, because he's not as good in school as I am. It still hurts.

The thing is, I don't think my father really wanted a girl. When I was little, he always tried to get me to play ball with him, but I was never very good at it. Then when my brother came along, he just kind of ignored me. My mother says that's normal, that fathers always like their sons best, because they know how to play with them. But I still think it's not fair that I have to be perfect and my brother gets away with murder. I mean, I have feelings, too. Sometimes I really hate my father.

High School Pressures
by Julie Stillman

I don't want to be mean but . . .

I have a bit of a problem. It's about this friend of mine, Lisa. Lisa and I have been friends since grammar school. When we began junior high school, we began drifting apart. We both made new friends, she got involved in schoolwork, and I became a real social butterfly. We spoke a little in school, but rarely on the phone. We'd get together once in awhile, but I was just an average twelve-year-old girl, and I was embarrassed to tell my friends that I had gotten together with her. Everyone thinks she's a nerd and a loser.

The summer before beginning our freshman year in high school, all my popular friends were away on vacation with their families or visiting relatives or at summer camp. I got bored hanging around by myself, so I decided to call Lisa. I asked her to come to the movies, and she agreed. We had a terrific time at the movies. She seemed like she had matured since the last time I had hung out with her.

The next day, Lisa called me, and we talked for awhile, and then decided to have a sleepover at her house. For the next couple of days, Lisa would keep calling me, asking if I wanted to do something with her. I usually said yes. We had a really great summer spending time with each other, and at the end of the summer, Lisa invited me to go with her family to Cape Cod for the weekend. I was so excited! I could not wait. We had a terrific time at the beach, in town, everywhere.

School started a few days after we got home. The first day of school was the first time I'd seen my other friends in over three-and-a-half weeks. We were all so excited to see each other that I didn't pay any attention to Lisa. My friends don't like Lisa, so they tried to keep me away from her. I don't know how to tell her, without being mean, that I can't always be with her, and she can't count on me to be her best friend like the old days. It's so hard being in high school. There's so much liking and disliking that you don't know how to handle situations. So my final decision is, I'll just have to explain to Lisa that it's just not going to work. I hope she understands. I really, really hope she doesn't hate me! I'm really not trying to be mean . . .

Homework
by Leslie Reed

I was in the kitchen doing my homework. Everything around me was white. All the appliances were shiny, even in the shadows. The only light was above the table, where I was sitting with my school books in front of me. I was writing in my notebook. I could see through the sliding glass doors that it was dark out. The clock said eight o'clock.

My Dad was there, pacing back and forth past the refrigerator. He looked very violent. He yanked the refrigerator door and took out a bottle of soda and poured himself a glass. His nostrils were flaring, his eyes red and bulging. He was mumbling. There was a lump on his forehead, and it seemed to be getting bigger the angrier he got. He looked at me and said in a very loud and angry voice, "Where is that bitch? She was supposed to be home hours ago." I felt myself crumple into a little ball, and I could hear myself saying, "I don't know." He kept pacing, and I tried to go back to my books, but he yelled again, and I jumped back to attention. "I don't believe that woman," he yelled. "She said she was going to drop something off at Mrs. Coppola's, and that was three hours ago. That fucking bitch, she must have gone shopping or something. Where the hell is she, God damned fucking bitch?"

He kept screaming and looked at me as if I were her. I felt powerless and afraid. I wanted to get away from the table, but I felt trapped. I was frozen. He gulped the soda down and opened the refrigerator again. He grabbed some cold cuts and stuffed them into his mouth, chewing with his mouth open like an animal at the kill. Then he slammed the refrigerator shut and came toward me, still chewing. I thought he was going to kill me. But he went right past me and pulled the sliding door open with such force that the door shattered all over him and all over the floor. Still yelling about "that bitch," he raced out of the kitchen and went upstairs to his room. I just sat there in the dim light and looked at the thousand tiny bits of glass that were all over the floor.

Candy
from *Street Kid*
by David Mead

Okay! You win. My name is Parsons, Janie Parsons. I come from Boulder, Colorado. I've been in town for about a year. On the street about eleven months. Both my parents are dead, and there are no relatives. None that wants me. I'm 17. Really, I am!

What about Shadow? I didn't meet Shadow. You don't meet Shadow. He meets you. Usually in the bus station. At least, that's where I met . . . he met me. I was having breakfast at the McDonald's, and he sat down next to me. We got to talking. He asked if I knew anybody. I didn't, so he offered to put me up for the night. Dumb, huh? Well, maybe not so much. I was down to my last five bucks. I needed a place to hang out. And he was sharp-looking. You know, not handsome or a hunk or anything, but sharp. And he talked that rappin' street talk, and I thought he was pretty cool. So I went with him. And then I stayed with him for a month. And he was nice. I mean it, real nice! He didn't hit me or anything, and he made me feel good. Then about a month after I'd been there, at his place, he told me I had to leave. It wasn't nasty or anything. He was real sorry to make me go, but he said he couldn't afford to keep me any longer. Something about his payments getting higher, or his rent going up. Some shit like that. So I said I'd go to work, help pay for my keep. But I couldn't do nothing. I didn't know how. I tried to get work, but nobody would hire me. I was underage. I did try, though. For two solid weeks I tried. Then I came home one night. I think it was the first week in January. I was all frustrated and pissed off, because I couldn't get work. And Shadow was there . . . with a friend. A big, good-looking guy. Shadow called him

Punch. And he was a hunk. I mean, my jaw just hit the floor looking at him. Anyway, we got to talking, and he said he liked my looks. Like "sugar candy" ready to lick. By that time, I was getting the picture. I thought about getting mad. About slugging Shadow. But something stopped me. It wasn't fear. I wasn't afraid of Shadow. I was a little of Punch, but not Shadow. He was a 100 pound weakling.

But I was thinking about where I would go and what I could do. I got up and went into the next room. I started packing. Shadow came in after me. He tried to talk me into staying. I told him to go fuck himself. He told me I'd starve. That I wouldn't last ten days unless I started working the streets. And if I did that on my own, I'd get ripped off or sliced up or maybe killed. I threw something at him. I don't remember what. Then I started to cry.

That night I slept with Punch. And I slept with Punch once a week for the next couple of months. By then, I was full time on the street. You're thinking it, aren't you? Another stupid, little cunt. A dumb country bitch gets took by some quick-talking nigger pimp. But I wouldn't be here if it wasn't for guys like you. You and all those other do-gooders out there. People who have ideas about how everybody else should live and act and dress. You're the bastards who ought to be locked up. Shadow's only trying to make a living. And he protects me. He runs off guys that look psycho, and he pays off the beat cop. And he got me out of Juvenile twice, put up the bail and everything. He doesn't take too much of my earnings either. A fair price for the work he does. And where was I going to go anyway?

I hate the street. But it's better than Boulder. You know what a virgin is in Boulder, Colorado? Any girl who can run faster than her stepfather.

Monologues
for
Boys

Planet "W"
by Keith Gooberman

Once there was a planet "W." I was the first astronaut that landed on planet "W" in 1933, when I was twenty-two years old. It was amazing that I was alive when I got back to Earth. I was the first person to go to planet "W" for two weeks and come back. It was so amazing, because planet "W" is not that pleasant, because snakes have boxing gloves on their slime tails. And the mice have teeth that are made from nails, and they bite. There are also envelopes that try to suck you up and send you to planet "X." And planet "X" is worse than planet "W," because you can't leave planet "X" and you can leave planet "W."

And anyway, the Vobsters keep you hostage. The Vobsters are aliens that have 8 eyes, 2 mouths, 4 nostrils and 2 necks. The way I know how they look is, they paint their pictures. Then they send their pictures to planet "W" and hang them up on rocks at planet "W." When I got back to Earth, I had a party at Nickelodeon Studio. I also got tickets to the World Trade Center. I had so much fun that my eyes popped out!

My Life So Far
by Alex Merkler

When I was two-and-a-half, my teacher was Ms. Graham. She was very small, but she was always nice. I was very quiet, and I hardly said a word. I always wanted to take the bus, but I couldn't take it, because I lived two blocks away from the school. I also cried a lot, because I didn't want to leave my Mommy.

When I was three years old, I had Ms. Bishop. She left in the half year to have a baby. I remember, she had a big stomach. Her assistant took over. She was Spanish.

When I was four and five, I had Ms. O'Conner. She was very tall and thin, and I counted up to two thousand five hundred fifty four. I also remember talking about fire drills. Just at that moment, the bell rang for a fire drill. When I went down the stairs, I was a little scared, but not much.

Then in kindergarten, I had Ms. Mintz. We did our homework in school, and she had bright orange-red hair. We put on the play, *The Elephant's Child*. That was a lot of fun. Ms. Mintz was sometimes strict.

In first grade, I was six and seven years old. I was wilder, and I talked more. My teacher was Ms. Athanassiades. Ms. A. was always nice, except for one day, she and Ms. Kamlet dressed up as Viola Swamp, and boy, were they mean!

In second grade, I was seven and now I'm eight years old. I still have Ms. A. We get more homework. We do more reading and writing, and I made a lot of flags this year.

I entered school when I was a baby, and now I feel grown up.

The Revival Meeting
by Marsh Cassady

We're having revival services. And these two weird people are here. I hate them. They're two sisters. They're horrible and they're ugly. They're fat and have black hair pulled into knots behind their heads. They always dress in black. They have hairy moles on their faces. I heard them in church Sunday morning, and then we went back again Sunday night.

The only thing I liked in church was when they lit a cigarette and stuck it in a rubber tube with a bulb at the end, and the tube stuck through a dummy's mouth. They squeezed the bulb, and the dummy smoked. This was just so they could say how bad cigarettes are. That was funny. But then they started to sing their stupid songs and yell at everyone to be saved.

I hate to hear their voices. They're loud and mean and keep shouting about hell. They sing together, "Jesus is calling thee tenderly home, calling today, calling today . . ." If Jesus is calling me tenderly, why do the ugly sisters scream their songs? One of them went through the whole church and whispered to people and asked whether they were saved or not. She walked up to my Dad and told him he was going to hell. She's a stupid old witch. No! I can't think that. It's bad. But I go to Sunday school and church, too. I know better than this old hag. There, I did it again. Aunt Helen said never to call anyone a hag. But this dumb old hag's a hag. Dad goes to church, and he's good. I hate her. My Dad isn't going to hell.

A Special Friend
by John Woodson

I know this midget. He's a man like my Dad, but he's only a little taller than me. And when I first saw him, I got scared, 'cause he was walking right towards me, and I could see he was a man and not a kid like me. And he must of could tell I was scared, 'cause he smiled at me and asked me my name and told me his name was Francis and said he knew my Dad and he used to be in the circus. And I said my Dad was, too. He trained all the elephants for Ringling Brothers. And I knew all the clowns. And Francis said he knew them, too, and then we smiled at each other.

And after that we smiled and said "hi" to each other every time we saw each other. And the kid who lived next door started to make fun of me, 'cause he saw me talking to a midget. And this kid — well, he's not a kid, he's like thirteen or so, and his Dad drives a big truck that is always cold in the back. And one day, we were just playing army or something — 'cause he would play army with us — and he captured me and put me in his fort, which was his Dad's truck, and then locked the door and kept me in there for a long time and wouldn't let me out. And the truck was freezing and no one could hear me. And then everyone must have gone home to supper, 'cause I could tell from this little crack that it was dark, and I was real scared and I was crying. And finally the door opened, and there was Francis with my Mom and this kid and his Dad. Boy, his Dad sure hit him, and I never spoke to him again. Francis made sure I got home safely with my Mom, because she was so worried, her eyes were all red.

The True Story of the Big Bad Shark
by China Millmin

It's not fair! Why does everyone blame me? Big sharks are supposed to eat little fish!

Now, I know what you're thinking. You're thinking that I should have controlled my appetite. But what was I supposed to do? Break the food chain or something? I mean, they didn't even listen to my side of the story. That's why you're here.

I was just swimming along Sand Bar Street, when suddenly I realized that I was hungry. I was on a diet, so I decided to go over to the local salad bar, when I saw Wild Willy, my biggest enemy, making a play for my girlfriend, Sheila Shark! Now, that made me very mad, so I did an incredibly dumb thing. I picked a fight with Wild Willy. But Sheila really hates fighting, so she said that instead of fighting, whoever brought her the tastiest fish would be her guy. We agreed.

I headed over to Coral Cove, where the tastiest fish hang out. Everybody knows that the tastiest fish in our side of the sea was Sweet Sarah. The only problem was that she was also the prettiest and was always surrounded by piranha. I had to find Sarah when she was alone.

I finally came up with a plan. Sarah always spent her lunch hour alone, because she insisted on privacy when she ate. Well, my plan worked. I successfully snuck into Silly Sandy's Snack Bar, where Sarah has lunch, and disguised myself as a waiter. And I did it! I grabbed Sweet Sarah and made a run for the door. Suddenly, the Piranha Police jumped out and grabbed me.

The next few days went by in a blur. I was taken to court and arrested for fishnapping. The day after I went to jail, I called my pal, Terry Tuna — he's a TV news photographer — and told him my story. He yelled, "Sweet Sarah was my girlfriend!" Then he hung up on me. How was I supposed to know that Sweet Sarah was his girlfriend? Anyway, I just wanted to ask if he could get my story on the six o'clock news.

Say, do you know anyone at CBS?

The Pitcher
by Jeffrey Fernandez

When my father was a young boy, he liked the Yankees. He remembers when they would mostly win every day, or when someone would hit a home run to win the game in the late innings. When I think of it, I wish I was born so I could have watched the game with my father. My father said that when he was in school, the 1956 World Series was going on, and when school was over, he ran home to see the game. In that game, the pitcher for the Yankees pitched a perfect game. He told me great stories about a guy that played for the Yankees named Mickey Mantle. When I hear this name, I think of a power machine, because he was so good.

Another story that my father told me was one day in a game, the "power machine," Mickey Mantle, hit a home run that went out of the stadium and across the street in a lumber yard. One day I hope someone makes a time machine, so people can go back in time to see things that went on. So, if someone does make a time machine, I will pick to go back and see the baseball games that my father saw. "Chris Chambliss hits home run to win the pennant for the Yankees in 1976," says the record books. I wonder how great he must have felt to hit that home run and do something great for the team.

When I get older, I want to be a baseball player for the New York Yankees. I will always keep my dream to be a pitcher or first baseman. Every day I think about it, and I hope my dream will come true. Maybe I will be in the record books one day, and if I am, I will remember it for the rest of my life.

The Diet Starts in the Store
by Trent Jones

When I was fat, I was eating a lot. I had all kinds of candy. This was before I was on my diet. I was eating chocolate chips and other weird stuff. When I was eating like that, I was getting fatter. I weighed 150 pounds. Kids made fun of me, and I was getting into fights. I had a sickness called sleep apnea caused by my fatness. I had to go to the hospital for an operation. I got mad at myself for weighing 150 pounds.

My mother helped me to overcome the kids making fun of me. Also, she used to work at Weight Watchers. She said, "Hey, Trent, why don't you go on the Weight Watchers diet?"

Now I am on my diet. I can eat, but not like before, not as much.

I had someone to talk to. Her name was Kathy. She was my psychologist. She was very intelligent, loving. It was almost like she was a mother to me. Before I could say anything, she knew what I was going to say. My mother and Kathy talked and talked.

I was tempted when I saw cookies and other stuff. I learned something from my mother and my aunt — that if I buy a cookie, I would be kidding myself. Because if I buy it, that automatically means I'm going to eat it. So the diet starts in the store, you know what I mean? If you have a problem like the one I had, remember my story. It's still an uphill climb, but I'm getting very good results.

Halloween
by John Woodson

Halloween, my Mom let me be anything I wanted, so I wanted to be a hobo like I heard my Dad talk about, and I miss him, 'cause he isn't around a lot lately — he's somewhere looking for work. So I get to be a hobo, and I find these really old pair of my brother Lloyd's jeans and an old flannel shirt of my Dad's and some rope for a belt and a pair of old boots. But the really great part is that I burn this cork and then I rub it all over my chin and face, and I got a beard like the real hobos have. And then I tie a bandanna on a stick, and I even take some clothes and stuff them in the bandanna that's on this stick, and I am ready to go trick-or-treating.

I started on our side of the street, so I could pass the old witch's house in the light. Yeah, she's a real witch. They live just across the street and one house up, and they have all this stuff in the yard, like refrigerators, car parts, boxes, statues and stuff, and I know she uses them for her witch's stuff. And her kids, they don't go to school. And I know she's a witch, 'cause at night sometime I heard her cackle like a witch and then run outside and chase her kids. And they also go number two outside, so I don't want to pass their house on this night in the dark.

But right after that house is this really nice people's house, but I think something happened. Well, I got to their house, and Mr. Miller let me in, and they were sitting on the sofa that faced the door, and in front of them was a big wooden bowl of candy bars. And they told me I could have as many as I wanted, and would I please trick-or-treat them. And I did, and they laughed, 'cause I told them about Superman and Batman and the Ninja Turtles. And they smiled and said I could have as many candy bars as I wanted, 'cause no one else was gonna come by. And then they said good-bye, and she held my hand for a long time, and I think she started to cry. And then he smiled at me, and I went home with all my goodies.

The next morning, I could tell my Mom was upset, and I thought it was because I ate too much candy, but that didn't seem to be it. I asked her, and she said, did I remember going to the Millers last night, and I said yes, 'cause they were really nice, and they gave me as much candy as I wanted. And she asked me when, and I said right before I came home. And then a policeman came to our door, and he had his gun and all this neat stuff, and my Mom told him what I just said. And then they talked real quiet for a minute, and then the policeman left, and Mom said that Mr. and Mrs. Miller were no longer with us, 'cause a real bad thing happened right after I left, and did I see any guns. And I said no. And later, I found out that Mrs. Miller hung herself right after she said good-bye to me practically, and Mr. Miller called up his next door neighbor to come over, and when he opened the door, a gun shot Mr. Miller on the couch. He rigged it up, and the neighbor felt, well, you know, terrible.

My Grandpa
by Marsh Cassady

My Dad was the youngest out of sixteen kids, so my Grandpa was really old when I was born. One of my teachers at school thought he was my great grandpa. He had a white beard. He lived way out in the country, and I liked to go to his house to listen to his stories.

He told about how he used to go all over the mountains to trap furs. One time, he slept by a log and woke up to see a bear standing beside him. And another time, a copperhead snake bit him, but he didn't die. He told Mom and Dad and me that he even remembered when President McKinley was shot. I could hardly believe that, but he was just a little boy then. His own Dad drove a stagecoach between Bedford and Somerset.

One time, he spent the whole winter trapping in the snow. He got a lot of skins and sold them and then came home. It was very late at night. He had a lot of money and was afraid someone would steal it. So he hid it down inside the stove. It was an old stove that burned wood he always chopped. Anyhow, that night it got cold. Grandma got up to fix breakfast and started a fire. She burned up all the money.

Grandpa was out chopping wood one day and had a heart attack. I was eight years old then. He died right away — at least that's what Dad said. I miss him. And I try to keep thinking about the stories he told me. But I can't remember a lot of them.

Surprise Party
by Marsh Cassady

Mom had a surprise party for me last year on my birthday. I was sixteen. She sent me to Rick's house to ask if he'd like to go out to dinner and then to a movie to help celebrate. When I was gone, the other kids came to the house. All my friends from school.

Rick and I walked into the living room, and everyone yelled, "Surprise." Then we went to the grove out back to build a fire for a wiener roast, and I started to open my presents. We heard a loud crash and ran to the highway. There was a car in the field up the hill. We ran to see if we could help. The car had crashed through a barbed wire fence and was laying upside down. A man screamed, "My legs! Oh, my God, my legs!" He was on the driver's side, and someone sat beside him. The roof was crumpled, and we couldn't tell anything about the other person, just that his chest was covered with blood.

Someone said that maybe we should try to get the two men out, because the car might explode. Rick said, maybe we should wait for an ambulance. Then the driver started to cry. "Please, fellows," he said. "Oh, God, please." So Bob said we should place ourselves around the car, and he called out, "One, two, three, lift."

I was on the passenger side, and Jesus God, this guy was lying there with his head against the roof. And his head was cut off, hanging from a little bit of skin in back. I started to puke and choke, but somehow I held onto the car. A couple of my friends pulled the other man out. His legs were smashed and twisted all weird-like. Someone ran to call an ambulance, and we all went back home, except for Bob, who said he'd wait till the ambulance came.

We were all sitting around in the living room, not talking or anything. And one of the girls — Sally, I think it was — said that since the fire was going good out back, we might as well have our wiener roast. So we all went out there and tried not to think about the guys up in the field. We heard the siren when the ambulance came.

We sat around the fire, and it was almost dark, and we tried to pretend that nothing had happened. It's almost a year now, and I can still see this guy's head just hanging there and the blood. And I'll always remember my sixteenth birthday.

Monologues
for
Girls
or
Boys

Ice Skating
by Dorell Edwards

My story.

This story is about my trip to the ice skating rink. It took place today. I can skate pretty good, but nothing like Michelle Kwan or Brian Boitano or like Midori Ito. They're professional ice skaters. Anybody who can skate like that has great talent, not meaning other activities aren't good, but that just came to my mind that moment. While I was there, I saw Levar Burton, the host of *Reading Rainbow*. Besides, of all the other things I've done there, I had a great time.

The end.

To the Rescue
by Danielle C. Miller

One day last summer, I went to Wildwood Crest. I went out in the ocean very far out with my raft to ride the waves. Suddenly a huge wave tossed me into the water and threw my raft into the surf. The current pushed me out away from the shore. I started to panic, because I saw the lifeguard coming to rescue me. But the waves were so big, it made it hard for him to get to me. I swallowed some water, and I thought I was going to drown. Then the lifeguard saved me. Ever since then, I never went out that far without a parent.

Being Sad
by Kisha Sutton

The most saddest day of my year when I was 5 is when I heard my grandfather died. He died on Abraham Lincoln's birthday. He died of cirrhosis of the liver. When it was his funeral, I was too sad and frightened to go to his funeral. Instead, I went to school. I shouldn't of had went to school, because all day, I was crying hard. At all times. It was pitiful. I got over it, but every time it's Abraham Lincoln's birthday or my grandfather, Assten Meekins' birthday, I go visit his grave and cry more and more for days.

Valentine's Day
by Jessica Morales

The most important thing that happened to me was what happened to my mother. On February 4, she had a fever of 106, and her heart stopped every four seconds. What made it worse was that she has Lupus.

On that night, I came home from school, and she was on the couch shaking, and she was very pale. When they called the ambulance, I had to go to my aunt's house. When the ambulance came, they took my mother, and my uncle and grandmother went with them. Three days later, my mother was better. My grandmother told me that she was going to try to let me see my mother, and it worked. My mother was happy when she saw me. On Valentine's Day, she came back home.

That is the very important thing that happened to me, and that is why Valentine's Day is so special to me.

The Baby Mouse
by Jessica Krueger

There was once two mice. One of the mice was called Allison, and the other was Richard. Allison and Richard were married. So, after their honeymoon, Allison wanted to have a baby. Richard agreed. And soon Allison got fatter and fatter, but it wasn't because she ate too much — it was because she was going to have a baby!

Soon the day came that the baby was born. And right when his head came out, he sneezed. Now, Allison was so worried, because she thought babies weren't supposed to sneeze right when they were born. Richard said that it was probably allergies. And boy, was he right! After that sneeze, he sneezed again. And soon, Allison and Richard found out that he was allergic to blood.

When Allison, Richard and the baby got home from the hospital, they found out that the baby was allergic to flowers. He was also allergic to grass, beans, eggs, leaves, the smell of ink, the smell of crayons, poison ivy, poison oak and stuffing. Sounds a little ridiculous, right? But it was true. And after all that, they named their little tyke Little Sneezer.

Mr. Universe
by Lee Sharmat

When I turned eleven, my brother, Sam, came home and brought me presents. I was very surprised, because I always thought he hated me. He teased me about everything, 'specially when he caught me on the toilet one morning with the door open. He even almost hit me once. He was bugging out on pot, and we were fighting over who would use the phone. He pulled it away from me and hit himself in the chin.

Mom said he was sick, and they thought I didn't know what it was, but I did. I learned about it in school. It's AIDS. I know all about it. It's about sex and drugs and blood stuff. Mom nearly feel over when I said this. I know kids who fool around already, but they think it's funny. This girl, Mara, isn't even a virgin anymore, I think. She did it with Stuart. All the boys like her, 'cause she's got big titties. I don't know — I mean, I know about sex. I even know how two boys do it, and I mean, I think it's weird, but whatever.

So they brought in this hospital bed — that's what Mom calls it — and tubes and shit and, like, attacked Sam, and I knew he didn't want it, but no one would listen 'cept me, and Mom dragged me out.

I told Sam I knew he had AIDS, and I saw how skinny he was with no shirt on. He used to be fat. That was before Mom told him to go away.

I woke up one night, and I could smell fried eggplant. Mom cooks it sometimes, so I went down to the kitchen, 'cause I wanted some. Usually she yells at me, 'cause she wants it all, but she didn't, and then she told me to finish it. She never did that! So I ate the eggplant and licked the plate clean, just like she does. I asked Mom if she had safe sex, and she cracked up and said she had no sex. But then she said that I should listen to that stuff I hear in school, because she's too shy to tell me.

I asked her if Sam was gonna die like Ryan White. And Mom was shaking her head, and then she was crying. Wow! Never seen Mom cry before. And I didn't know what to do, so I cried, too. And you know what? Then she talked to me and told me everything, and then I told Sam everything Mom told me. And he laughed and then spit up all this shit, and I knew he was gonna die.

Sam had to go to the hospital, and Mom didn't want me to go, but I yelled, so she snuck me in. I knew why Sam didn't want to go. It smelled funny, and they kept him all tied down. And lots of machines and beeping noises like on TV. The nurse came in and got all mad, because I wasn't supposed to be there. And then I got mad, and Mom got mad, and we were all jumping around. And then the nurse left. I told Sam I loved him and gave him a big hug.

I was in Math class. Mara was passing a note to Jeffrey, and kids were talking, but I kept on staring at the lines between the fractions. And then, Mr. Costello, the principal, came in and waved at me. And everyone was looking at me, and I just knew that Sam died.

No more watching him tie his shoes. Or getting mad at me. Or yelling at Mom and telling her to fuck off. Or dropping dishes. Or catching him posing in front of the mirror like Mr. Universe. Or making too many phone calls. Or coming in too late and Mom freaks out 'cause she thinks he's dead. And no more hugs or kisses or stupid stuff. No more nothing from Sambo, my bro, who I thought hated me but didn't, and I love him tons.

So I got up and I walked up front, and I knew the

principal wasn't going to say nothing. So I said, "You don't know nothing! My brother is dead from AIDS!" And everyone got real quiet, and I felt good, because maybe they'd stop laughing, because it's me they've been laughing at and Sam who's dead.

And I was at the cremation thing where they've burned up Sam. And Dad is there, which is good, feeling bad for not seeing Sam more, which is good, too.

You know, when I got home, I'd missed school for that week, and there was a big box downstairs, and I brought it by Sam's bed and opened it, and it was all cards from class, including Mara and Jeff and Stuart and everyone. But I cried, because I know Sam is gone forever.

Maybe I'll make eggplant, if Mom will let me try. Maybe I'll let her have some, too.

For the Love of Acting
by Sierra Millman

I first saw live actors on stage when I was six or seven years old. Entering the theater, I remember huge oak staircases, loud salesmen selling T-shirts, and dusty velvet curtains. These things made me nervous, and I couldn't wait to get to my seat, so I could shrink down and disappear into the folds of the chair. We were late. My mother took my arm and lightly propelled me through the crowded foyer and up to the balcony.

I remember everything — the sweet scent of my mother's perfume, every movement of the actors and actresses as they waltzed, pirouetted or walked gracefully across the stage. I was so captivated by the performance, when it was over, I continued to sit and stare in awe at the blackness of the empty stage, so filled with life, beauty and drama a few minutes before.

For weeks, I stood in front of the mirror, copying each gesture, each line I could remember. I wanted so much to be like those performers. Parading across my "stage," constructed of a couple of cardboard boxes and a long wooden board, I made up small plays of my own, often employing my family as an audience. They were very patient with me.

In seventh grade, I finally found the courage to audition for a dramatic performance. At the audition, a part of me wished that I could again shrink down into the safety of one of the plush seats in the audience. When I stepped up on stage, my knees began to tremble and my mouth felt dry. I had a difficult time starting to speak, afraid that if I opened my mouth, no sound would emerge. I began to read with a stutter at first, but as I continued, I felt more comfortable. I had picked up a funny accent that seemed to fit my character. The other students laughed at my performance, but not in a bad way.

A week later, I ran to the drama room to see the cast list posted on the wall. I got the part! Along with the rest of the cast, I rehearsed for many weeks. I had such a joyous time at rehearsals, I felt sad when they ended.

Then came our first performance, and something magical happened: When I stepped out on stage and saw the audience staring up at me — when I spoke my first line — I became the character. I spoke as though I was saying those words and feeling those emotions for the first time. I was not myself that night. When I first walked out on that stage and felt the heat of the lights and heard my own voice, I felt as though I had come home. I felt as though I would live forever. And when I made my final exit, I was walking on air. All worries were nonexistent, all troubles forgotten, for I knew that as long as the stage remained, I could escape. As long as the stage remained, I would never die.

NOTES

NOTES

NOTES

Ordering Information

To order additional copies of *By Kids, For Kids*, just send $7.95 per book plus $2.50 postage/handling for the first book and $1.00 for each additional book (New York State residents, please add sales tax) to:

Excalibur Publishing Inc.
511 Avenue of the Americas, PMB 392
New York, New York 10011

Checks and money orders should be payable to Excalibur Publishing. For credit card orders, please include type of card, your name as it appears on the card, card number, expiration date and your signature. Credit card orders can also be placed using our toll-free number, 1-800-729-6423.

For further information, to request a complete catalog, or for quantity orders, write to the address above or call 212-777-1790. Visit our web site at http://ourworld.compuserve.com/homepages /ExcaliburPublishing.

Other Monologue Books by Excalibur

By Actors, For Actors, Volume 1: A collection of original monologues and scenes

By Actors, For Actors, Volume 2: A collection of original monologues and scenes

By Actors, For Actors, Volume 3: A collection of original monologues and performance pieces

For additional information and a list of monologues and scenes, see our web site: http://ourworld .compuserve.com/homepages/ExcaliburPublishing.

About the Editor

For twenty-eight years, Catherine Gaffigan has worked in theatre, television and film as director, producer, actress and teacher. As an actress, she made her New York debut opposite Dustin Hoffman in *Journey of the Fifth Horse*. She toured the country for two years in *Cabaret*, played Lady MacBeth, did stints in summer and winter stock, made many television commercials, suffered the agonies of soap opera life, and appeared in both Broadway versions of *Whose Life Is It, Anyway?* Her films include *Julia* and Brian DePalma's thriller *Sisters*. Since 1971, she has taught Master Classes in Acting in her own New York studio. In 1987, she produced and directed the North American premiere of *Lady Susan*, based on the Jane Austen novel, for the Jane Austen Society. She subsequently directed *Deals and Deceptions, Restaurant Romances, An Evening of Hilarity and Hidden Agendas, The J.A.R.* (world premiere), *Dance Me to the End of Love, Tom and Viv* and *Murder in the Cathedral*. Catherine holds a BA in English from St. John's University and an MFA in Drama from The Catholic University of America. She also trained in the New York studio of James Tuttle.